Don't Lose Money!

(in the Stock Markets)

Tony Loton

LOTONtech

www.lotontech.com

Published by LOTONtech Limited (www.lotontech.com), printed and distributed by Lulu (www.lulu.com).

ISBN-13: 978-0-9556764-0-6

ISBN-10: 0-9556764-0-1

Contents

Acknowledgements

I'd like to thank all those who volunteered to review the original manuscript for this book; for no more reward than a mention here – and a free copy.

Those volunteers were Weng Ang (a financial advisor), Martin Minney (representing the target audience), and Malcolm Wheatley (a professional writer and editor).

Thank you to you all.

Don't Lose Money (in the Stock Markets)

Introduction

My inspiration for this book comes from the two rules for investing popularly attributed to Warren Buffett, one of the world's greatest investors.

My paraphrasing of those rules is as follows:

Rule 1 – Don't Lose Money!

Rule 2 – Don't forget Rule 1.

From all the stock market speculation books I've read in recent years one statement sticks in my mind; a statement to the effect that: in the absence of any other strategy, an investor who follows only those two rules will become very rich over time.

I know you want to make money, not just avoid losing it; but to emphasize how important the preservation of capital is, consider this. If your investment falls by 50% you'll need a 100% rise to get you back where you started.

The idea of not losing money seems particularly relevant as I write this. In the period July to September 2007 the financial markets have been shaken by a 'credit crunch' induced by a crisis in the US sub-prime lending market. In layman's terms – banks had made (home) loans to less credit worthy folks who then defaulted on those loans when interest rates rose; which meant that banks were less willing to lend money (even to each other); which meant that they had to raise money by other means such as by selling equities on the stock markets. So while this was more of a problem in the money markets than in the stock markets, there was a very noticeable knock-on effect.

Your $10,000 invested in the US Dow Jones index in mid-July 2007 would have been worth less than $8,700 in mid-August; a fall of almost 14% in the space of a month, requiring a subsequent increase of around 15% to get back the initial stake. The story was pretty much the same if your investment was tied to the UK FTSE 100, Paris CAC, or German DAX stock indexes.

How fortunate, then, that in that time I didn't lose any money. In fact I made a little, and was well positioned to take advantage of any subsequent recovery.

Although many books out there claim to unlock the secrets of how to win big by getting into the market at the right time, surprisingly few give more than a passing mention of how to get out of the market when things turn sour; or how to make sure you're not in too deep in the first place. Those are the sweet spots I aim to hit with this book.

In part it's about protecting yourself from the unexpected events that Nassim Nicholas Taleb describes as "black swan events" in his book – unsurprisingly titled – 'The Black Swan'.

Why would I tell you My Secrets?
There are no secrets!

All of the ideas, trading rules, and tips you'll read about in this book have been expressed in one form or another by traders with longer track records than mine.

What I've done is: read all of the trading / investing books I could find, tried out all of the ideas that they contain, and condensed the ones that work for me into a single book.

Don't Lose Money (in the Stock Markets)

I've done that for my own benefit as well as yours; to document for myself what I consider to be 'my trading system', and to make sure I follow it. It's quite well documented that the biggest challenge faced by a trader is not 'finding a system that works' but 'making sure he (or she) sticks to it'.

And remember that my intention is not to show you how to get rich as you play the markets (though you might), but to help you avoid getting poor in the process.

I'm not the first person to have thought of this, and I have drawn inspiration from other well-known works. There's a lot to be learnt by studying the real-life exploits and advice of past masters such as Larry Livingston (aka Jesse Livermore) in Edwin Lefevre's 'Reminiscences of a Stock Operator' and Nicholas Darvas in his book 'Wall Street, the other Las Vegas'. I also recommend Van K Tharp's 'Trade Your Way to Financial Freedom' in addition to any books on market timing / trend following.

Who is this book for?
I'm not a professional trader, and never have been. Nor have I (yet) made millions playing the markets.

My aspirations are more modest than that. I trade on-line every day from my home office using my own money, and my objective is simply to earn enough each month through trading to achieve financial freedom. That is, not to have to work for someone else.

Since I have bills to pay every single month, not losing the money that I already have is just as important to me as making some more.

This book is likely to appeal to like-minded people. People who'd like to have a go at making a living by beating the system, but who can't afford to fail. Or maybe you're retired and no longer need to make a living? You'd like to have some fun trying to grow your nest egg; but you don't want to lose it all. Or maybe you've been hurt by bad advice in the past; the kind of bad advice that I allude to later in *Chapter 8*, which motivated me to take control of my investment decisions.

The majority of my examples should be relevant to traders in the UK, USA, or anywhere else for that matter. As a general rule I've used US dollar ($) amounts in my generic explanations, to ensure maximum readership; and UK pound sterling (£) amounts in my real-life experience notes, because that's my home currency. It's the numbers that matter, not the currency.

Use of the terms Trading, Investing, and Speculating

You will see that in this book I've used the terms 'trading', 'investing', 'speculating', and 'betting' somewhat interchangeably. In each case my decision regarding which word to use has largely been down to which sounded best at the time.

Whereas some authors may draw a distinction between 'trading' and the more noble art (apparently) of 'investing' I try to draw no such distinction. Whatever we call it, we are merely speculating – or betting – that our purchases will be worth more when we come to sell them than they were when we bought them. If a prospective long term 'investment' falls in value soon after purchase, I might sell out immediately thus resigning it to be a short term 'trade'. If a short term 'trade' rises in value I might hold on for as long as I can – maybe even years – thus rendering it an 'investment'. And

Don't Lose Money (in the Stock Markets)

for all practical purposes the operation of my 'spread trading' (aka 'spread betting') account is materially no different from my regular trading and investment accounts.

How many times have you heard someone say the following?

"I don't mind that my trade in stock X is showing a loss because it's a good long term investment"

It's amazing how many short-term traders become investors when the price falls.

How I got here

I took my first tentative steps in share trading (hereafter referred to simply as 'trading') around the time of the new millennium, 1999 / 2000. In the seven or eight years since then I have read just about every book I could find on trading, investment, speculation, call it what you will – it's all the same thing to me. I've also made every mistake there is to make including 'trying to catch a falling knife', 'overtrading', and a few others that I'll allude to in subsequent chapters.

I've never lost too much money from those mistakes, but each one taught me a valuable lesson about what to do when things go wrong. I've learnt from my mistakes, and maybe you will too.

I've tried to incorporate as much of my real-life experience as possible, in the form of an Experience Note that you'll find in each chapter.

Until recently my trading had been a part time activity, undertaken at the same time as trying to hold down a more conventional career in IT.

Tony Loton

As an independent IT consultant I learnt a lot about running a one-man business, I worked with many blue-chip financial institutions (including stockbrokers and fund managers), and I published several books. Titles such as 'Web Content Mining with Java' and 'Professional Visual Studio 2005 Team System' may not have any obvious connection with trading, but on deeper inspection you would see that every one of my examples in those books was somehow connected with my real passion – financial trading.

For example: my implementation of a web portal that extracted share prices from financial web sites, aggregated them, and issued 'buy' or 'sell' recommendations; or my high level architecture for a stock trading platform linking a web front-end, through a set of stock trading web services, to third party market makers.

As I write this in 2007 I have no sources of income other than the fruits of my trading and publishing activities. So I'm practicing what I'm preaching, and well on my way to financial freedom.

Who knows? Someday soon I might hit the financial jackpot. In the meantime I won't lose my shirt!

Tony Loton, October 2007

Chapter 1 – Trade Indexes

To diversify or not to diversify, that is the question.

One school of thought suggests that diversification is a good thing, since if you spread your eggs across several baskets you are unlikely to lose them all. The other school of thought suggests that to maximize returns you should indeed put all your eggs in one basket... and watch that basket carefully.

In this book I'm more concerned with protecting returns than I am with maximizing them, so I'm very much in favor of diversification; providing I don't over diversify to the extent that I become a jack of all trades (no pun intended), master of none.

Individual Stocks vs. Indexes
I've seen the following quote attributed to Warren Buffett:

"Indexing is the best approach for 99% of all investors"

Having walked both the 'individual stock' path and the 'index' path I'd certainly place myself firmly within the 99%. Sure, I've experienced some lucky (yes, lucky) rises on individual stocks; and an equal number of unlucky falls.

So what's wrong with individual stocks?

They're simply too unpredictable. There are countless reasons why an individual stock may fall in price – unsound fundamentals, bad management, faulty or unpopular goods, scandal and fraud, or general market conditions.

Unlike the professional fund managers past and present – such as Peter Lynch, who advocates specialization in a few stocks that you follow closely in the hope that they will become "ten-baggers" – I simply do not have the time, expertise, or support staff to facilitate a proper assessment of company fundamentals, to interview a companies' senior management, to research the market penetration of goods or services, and to analyze the company-specific news stream. So any success I achieve with an individual stock is much more likely to be down to luck rather than judgment.

You'll see later, though, that it is possible to make money having no more advantage than sheer luck – providing you practice effective money management.

I can have a better stab at assessing 'general market conditions' which affect all stocks. I can see that the Dow Jones index is rising or falling, that interest rates are historically high or low, that property prices are at an all-time low, or that we're experiencing a 'bubble' which could burst at any time.

In the spirit of this book – which remember is about not losing money – I'd like to put my bias towards index investing more simply. While any one company might go bust, it's unlikely that every one of the companies in the index will.

Don't put down this book if you're a keen stock picker. Index investing is just one of the weapons in my armory to protect against losing money. My other weapons – trend following, stop orders, position sizing, lowering costs, straddles and strangles – may be equally applicable to the stock picker. Skip the rest of this chapter if you will, then read on.

Don't Lose Money (in the Stock Markets)

Indeed, index investing is not universally popular, and one of the classic criticisms of index investing is that it dooms you to achieving only 'average returns'. I'll take a look at what we can expect of average returns shortly; but first a personal experience note.

Experience Note

Early in my trading experience I committed one of the cardinal sins of trading – averaging down. At the height of the dot.com boom I noticed that several IT stocks had fallen in price a little, and naively thought that "what goes down must come back up". So I bought one of those stocks, and it fell some more. With the stock now even cheaper I bought some more, and it fell some more. Repeat a few more times, until the dot.com bubble bursts and the company goes bust. Final value of my holding: zero.

That experience taught me that what goes down can go down some more – possibly all the way to zero. Which is one reason why I don't invest in individual stocks, and if in a moment of weakness I ever did, I would certainly not try to average down.

The situation is somewhat different with indexes, of course, because it's highly unlikely that all 30 stocks of the Dow Jones Industrial Average or all 100 stocks of the FTSE 100 would simultaneously fall to zero. On the well-documented rare occasions that it has (almost) happened, there has been a subsequent recovery... eventually.

What's wrong with Average Returns anyway?

Many professional fund managers claim to be able to 'beat the index' if you invest with them. But they can't all do it all of the time, otherwise the index would no longer represent the 'average' that it's meant to represent. Everything else being equal, for every investor who outperforms the index there must be a complementary investor who underperforms.

So you can either:

- Try to guess who the outperformers will be, and invest with them. Good luck!

- Or simply accept the relatively risk-free 'average returns' of an index tracker fund.

Don't get too excited about the statement about the average returns being risk free. I don't mean that you cannot lose money; but that relatively you can't lose more than the average market participant if you 'buy and hold' through the ups and downs.

Actually I won't be advocating buying and holding blindly through all the ups and downs; as you'll see in later chapters. But for this argument in favor of indexing let's make that assumption for now.

So what can we expect the average returns to be?

Well, it turns out that calculating average stock market returns is not as straightforward as you might think.

We could divide today's value of the Dow Jones Industrial Average (about 13 000, see Figure 1) by the value as of five years ago (about 8 000), subtract 1, and divide by 5 get the average annual return of the past five years. That gives a rather healthy 12.5% per annum.

Don't Lose Money (in the Stock Markets)

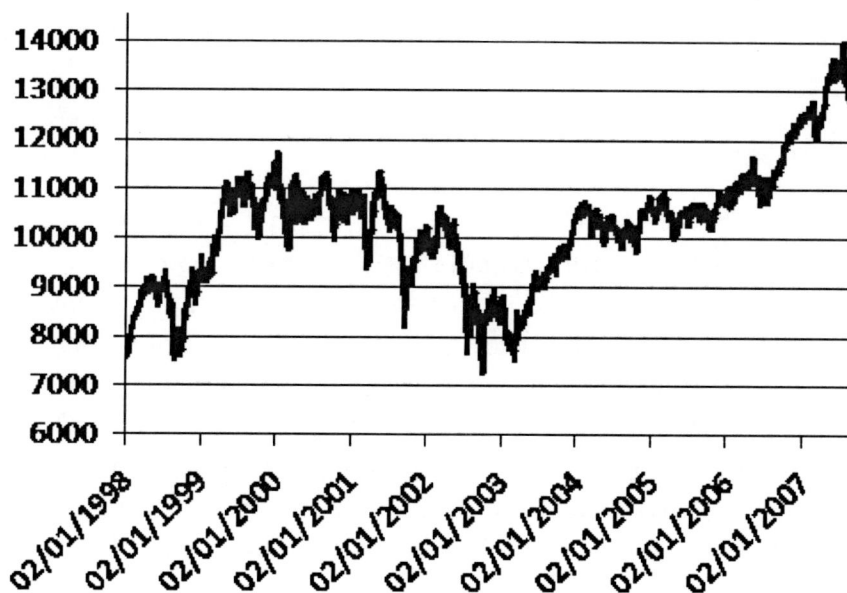

Figure 1 Dow Jones Industrial Average 1998-2007

There are several problems with that simple approach, including:

- The fact that the period 2002-2007 was a bull market; and a similar calculation for the immediately prior five years 1998-2002 (including the bursting of the dot.com bubble) would give a rate of approximately 0%. Still, the two combined would average out at 6.25%, which is not bad for simply buying and holding through bad times and good.

- The fact that we have performed a simple interest calculation, not a compound interest calculation that would use the equation **Value = Investment * (1+rate)^numberOfyears**. By rearranging that equation I can work out that an interest rate of 10.2% compounded over 5 years, or a rate of 4.97% compounded over 10 years would be required turn an investment of $8,000 into $13,000. *You can check my* *calculation using an on-line compound interest calculator such as the one at http://www.moneychimp.com/articles/finworks/fmfutval.htm.*

- The fact that dividend distributions have not been included in our calculations above. Each time a company pays a dividend, the share price is depressed by the amount of the dividend; but because the investor receives the dividend amount (minus tax), the money has not disappeared yet is not included in the increasing share price. So an investor's total return would be the increase in share price (or index value) plus the value of any dividends received. That could increase the investor's average returns by, for example, an additional 2.5% per annum.

Those calculations suggest that we might expect a compound annual return of 4.97% plus annual dividend income of around 2.5% = 7.47%. It turns out that the US Office of the Chief Actuary (OCACT), in common with financial institutions in the UK, suggests a figure of 7% for average stock market returns. So those of you thinking of buying and holding over a long period of time simply need to compare that 7% return with the interest rate offered by your savings account.

Now if you allow me a little artistic license in upping that rate slightly to 7.2% I can tell you that the 'Rule of 72' dictates that an interest rate of 7.2% will double your money every 10 years. So a $10,000 investment at age 20 would be worth $20,000 at age 30, $40,000 at age 40, $80,000 at age 50, and $160,000 at age 60. If you could hold out for retirement at age 70 you could have a nest egg amounting to $320,000.

Over the long term that rate of return should be relatively risk free because a) we've diversified across all stocks

Don't Lose Money (in the Stock Markets)

comprising the index, and b) we've accounted for bull and bear markets.

Now imagine how your returns could be improved if you invested your money elsewhere during the lost years 1998-2002 that yielded a 0% return (excluding dividends), or even better avoid the bear market years 2000-2002. You'll read more about that kind of 'market timing' in Chapter 2.

The Rule of 72
You might be wondering about the 'Rule of 72'; which I used in my argument, but didn't explain so as not to disrupt the flow. To estimate the time it will take to double your money invested at a given (compounded) interest rate, you divide 72 by the interest rate. For an interest rate of 10% your doubling time will be 72/10 = 7.2 years; for a rate of 7.2% your doubling time will be 72/7.2 = 10 years.

Having established that I'm an index investor, and (usually) not a stock picker, how do I put that index investing into practice?

Trading Indexes with ETFs
I trade indexes by buying and selling ETFs (Exchange Traded Funds); which are collective investments that are priced throughout the day like individual stocks, but which typically track major indexes.

I trade ETFs through three accounts that I hold with my stockbroker: A regular trading account, an ISA (tax-free Individual Savings Account), and a SIPP (Self Invested Personal Pension account).

Although I could trade traditional mutual funds or other collective investments through these accounts I have found that approach to be unsatisfactory because:

- Mutual funds tend to have an up-front fee ranging between about 1% and 5% of your initial investment. So you've lost a sizeable chunk as soon as you've committed, which you won't get back if you change your mind.

- Mutual funds are priced on a daily basis, and you have to wait up to 24 hours for a buy or sell instruction to be processed. So you can never be quite sure of the price you'll get when you sell.

- My trading accounts do not allow me to place stop orders (covered in Chapter 3) on mutual funds, so I can't sell out automatically if things turn sour.

In contrast, Exchange Traded Funds such as those listed by iShares (www.ishares.co.uk, www.ishares.com) provide the following benefits:

- There is no up-front fee; just the stockbroker's dealing charge and the bid-ask spread.

- They are priced continually throughout the day just like regular stocks.

- My stockbroker allows 'stop' and 'trailing stop' orders to be placed on ETFs.

Although iShares ETFs are provided by Barclays Global Investors, that doesn't mean you have to be a Barclays customer in order to trade them. The same iShares ETFs are available through numerous stockbrokers, and there are other providers of ETFs such as ProShares (www.proshares.com) and Deutsche Bank X-Trackers (www.dbxtrackers.co.uk).

My favorite ETFs, which you can look up on the iShares website, are iShares FTSE 100 (code ISF), iShares FTSE UK

Dividend Plus (IUKD), and iShares S&P 500 (code IUSA). Because the US housing property bubble seems to have burst as I write this, and there's a reasonable chance that the UK property market will go the same way, I'm also looking at the iShares FTSE EPRA/NAREIT UK Property Fund (code IUKP) and IShares FTSE EPRA/NAREIT US Property Yield Fund (code IUSP) for a recovery play in the future.

Those are my personal favorites, not specific recommendations for you. A more comprehensive sample list of ETFs is given in Appendix A – ETFs Sample List.

Trading Indexes with Spread Trading

I also trade indexes via my financial spread betting account.

I use the terms 'spread trading' and 'spread betting' interchangeably, as do the providers themselves sometimes. In my view, there really is no difference between trading and betting because every time you place a trade you're betting on a beneficial outcome for that trade. Even the noble art of 'investing' (as some like to think of it) can be considered to be betting – betting that your investment will grow (rather than shrink) over time.

My spread trading account is (at my request) a 'limited risk' account, which means:

1. I can only bet on the direction of major indexes such as Wall Street (i.e. US Dow Jones), FTSE (UK), CAC (France), and DAX (Germany); not individual stocks.

2. I cannot lose more money than I have on deposit in the account.

3. Each bet I place has a guaranteed stop loss order attached automatically. *You'll read about stop loss orders in Chapter 3.*

I chose a limited risk account with those restrictions because, as you know by now, I do like to trade indexes and I don't like to lose money!

Of the various types of spread bets on offer, I prefer 'rolling bets' that have no end date by which time the bet must have paid off.

Don't Over-diversify

You will have figured out by now that I concentrate mainly on the major UK and US indexes, with occasional forays into mainland Europe. Although I think it pays to diversify *within indexes* I don't think it's a good idea to diversify too much *between indexes*. By concentrating on just a few major indexes it is possible to get a feel for their characteristic ebbs and flows. Not so if you try to follow too many at once.

Referring back to the very beginning of this chapter, I prefer to put all my eggs (money) into one or two baskets (indexes) *and watch them carefully*.

Investing in Sectors

A more advanced technique would be to invest in specific market sectors – banks, telecoms, retail etc. – rather than whole markets (i.e. indexes). Sectors represent a halfway house between stocks and indexes: more specialist than indexes, less risky than individual stocks. Like indexes, market sectors have ebbs and flows that facilitate market timing (explained in Chapter 2).

At the time of writing a sector-based approach looks very attractive. As a knock-on effect of the US sub-prime crisis, a prominent UK mortgage bank has had to secure an emergency loan from the Bank of England. Its share price has been dented massively, and I mean <u>massively</u>, with every other UK bank following it downwards to some degree. While that particular stock looks attractive now, its future as a viable business is not guaranteed. But since the Bank of England and the UK government cannot conceivably let all of the players in that sector fail, there may well be an opportunity here to bet on 'all banks' recovering their sympathetically-depressed share prices.

So what's stopping me?

Well, although the list of available exchange traded funds is growing all the time, I can't find one as specific as the 'UK Banking Sector ETF'. The only option therefore would be to set up a DIY sector fund, by investing a modest amount in each of the ten-or-so separate banks. Ten separate investments incur ten sets of transaction fees; which I'll examine further in Chapter 4.

Don't Lose Money!

Remember to read on through the techniques that follow even if you're a stock picker. But for the record, I'm with Warren Buffett on this one in recommending that the majority of individual investors should...

Trade Indexes

Chapter 2 – Time the Market, Follow the Trend

In the previous chapter I established stock indexes as a safer alternative to individual stocks. I suggested that the average return achievable by buying and holding indexes for the long term is not so bad, but it's unlikely to have set you on fire.

In this chapter I'll look at how those average returns may be enhanced, and more importantly how losses may be reduced, by timing market entries and exits in order to catch the major up- and down- trends.

If you've not fully bought into my argument in favor of index investing, do stay tuned. Bear in mind that many successful market timers and trend followers apply these principles to individual stocks. In the discussion that follows just assume that my index price charts are price charts of individual stocks, and substitute my word 'index' for the name of your favorite stock. Not that I'm advocating investing in any stock or index simply because it's 'your favorite'.

Trend Following vs. Buy and Hold

According to Warren Buffett the ideal time to hold a stock (or index) is 'forever'.

Yes, that would be ideal since we would never have to manage our investments, never pay any transaction charges, and perhaps never pay any capital-gains tax. If all went according to plan with my investments, that's exactly what I'd do. But things don't always go according to plan.

Tony Loton

As we saw in Chapter 1, blindly buying and holding forces us to live through times of zero returns or even negative returns. Wouldn't you sleep more soundly if you were not invested during those times; but rather had your money sitting safely in cash earning a risk-free rate of interest?

Most of the financial advisers I've met over the years, especially the ones tied to a particular financial institution, advise that stock market investing is for the long-term.

"Leave your money with us for at least five years and you'll be alright", they say.

In Chapter 1 I demonstrated that over a long period the stock market should indeed yield a steady return... providing that the long period was not the five years between 1998 and 2002! Imagine that in 1998 you invested a lump sum in an equity-backed pension, five years before your retirement, only to find that your investment had not grown at all by the time you cashed in.

No, that's not for me. I'd like to benefit from the good times and avoid the bad. I'd like to time my entries and exits so as to ride an uptrend as long as possible, and then jump off when the tide turns.

The Potential Effect on Average Returns
In Figure 2 the line that I have superimposed shows the potential effect on returns by:

- Timing our entry into the market at the beginning of a major uptrend.

- Timing our exit, into cash, when the uptrend breaks.

- Timing our re-entry when a new uptrend establishes.

Don't Lose Money (in the Stock Markets)

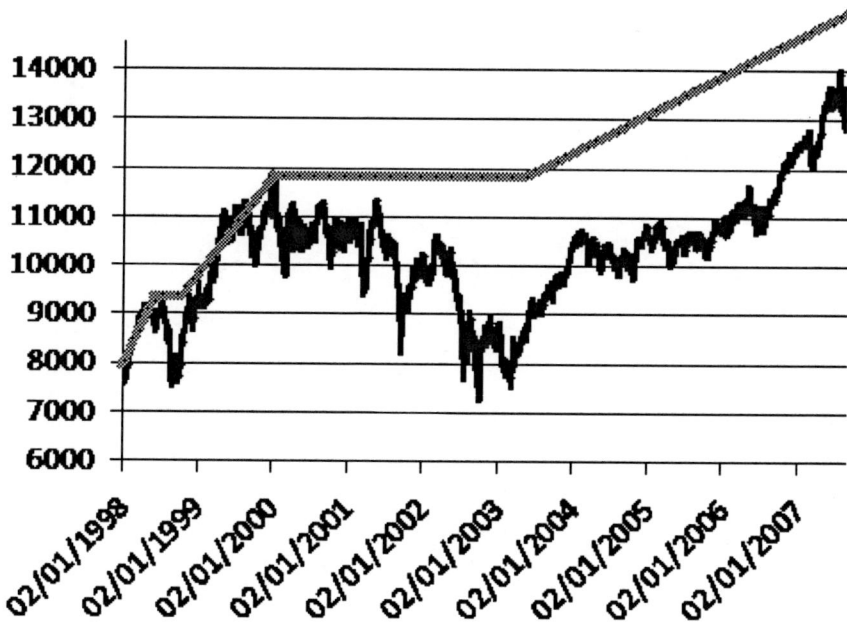

Figure 2 Potential Returns by Timing Entries and Exits

As you can see, my line ends at around what would be the 16 000 mark compared with final value of 13 000 for the index itself. Thus the total return over the whole period would be 100% compared with the total index return of 62.5%.

In Figure 3 the line that I have superimposed shows the potential effect on returns of:

- Buying long the market at the beginning of a major uptrend.

- Exiting, into cash, when the uptrend breaks.

- Selling short the market when a downtrend develops.

- Buying long the market when a new uptrend develops.

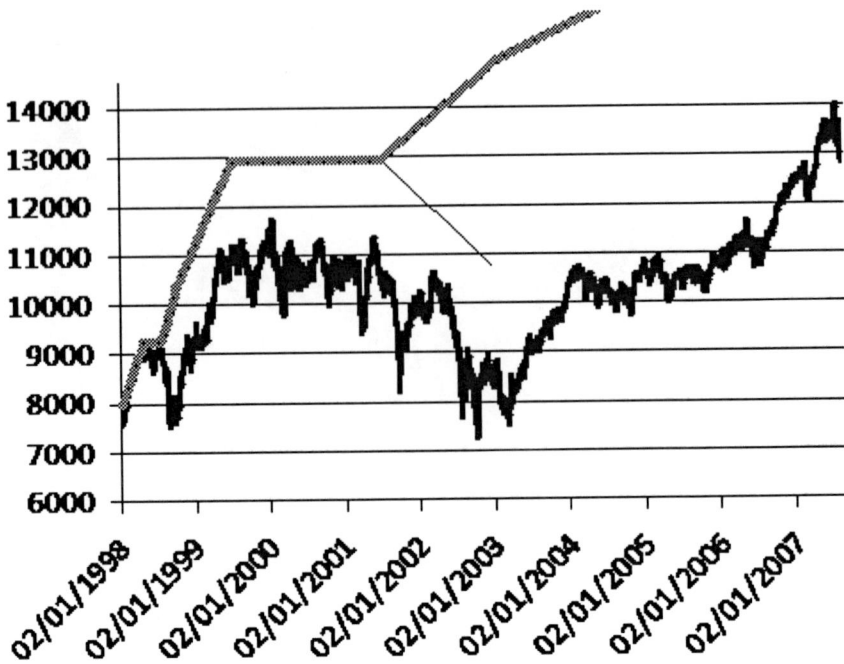

Figure 3 Potential Returns by Following UP Trends <u>and</u> DOWN Trends

A note about 'long' and 'short' trading
Trading LONG means BUYING a security (e.g. a stock or index ETF), and taking ownership of it, so as to benefit from any rise in price. Trading SHORT means SELLING a security that you don't own, so as to benefit from any price fall by buying it back later at the lower price. Don't worry about how you can sell something you don't already own; the stockbroker takes care of that.

The apparent advantage of that approach is that even when the market goes down, my line goes up. All the way off the scale!

You'll be thinking that there's big money to be made here; by focusing on 'when' to buy (market timing) rather than 'what' to buy (stock picking). Indeed we could turn my opening argument from the introduction on its head: if you invest in a market that has fallen 50% you'll make a 100% profit – double your money – when, or if, it fully recovers. But this book is not about making money; merely not losing it.

Whether you can take only long positions (speculating on an upward trend), or long and short positions (speculating also on a downward trend) will depend on the type of account you hold with your stockbroker.

My ISA account allows only long positions, my regular trading account and SIPP account both allow for short positions – of a sort – via Covered Warrants (explained in Chapter 6), and my spread trading account lets me bet either way (also Chapter 6) with equal ease. Beware, however, that covered warrants and spread bets are leveraged positions, which amplify any gains (great!) but also any losses (not so great!). So those wishing to limit their losses should perhaps stick with traditional long positions; which in my previous example still provides a healthy 100% return over five years.

Either way, what my examples clearly demonstrate is that by investing in indexes, and with a little timing and trend following thrown in, we need not be condemned to achieving 'average returns'. And regardless of how quickly the lines in my figures go up, they never go down, so we don't lose money.

Those idealized pictures show the theoretical potential, but it's not so easy in practice to spot the market turning points. As often quoted...

"No-one rings a bell at the top and bottom of the market"

Market Timers and Trend Follows

In his book 'All About Market Timing' Leslie Masonson suggests a set of ten technical indicators, and five trading strategies, to assist with predicting when the market will turn up or down.

Michael Covel, in his book 'Trend Following', suggests that it is virtually impossible to predict the twists and turns of the stock market but that it is possible to react to them. It's all about price action; that is, if prices are going up you should buy, and if prices are going down you should sell.

Whether predictive or reactive, what both have in common is that they are essentially 'technical' approaches that consider price movements, average prices, price volatility and so on. Neither approach advocates analyzing individual stocks' price / earnings ratios or other fundamentals; neither advocates blindly 'buying and holding'.

Two of the greatest traders of all time, Nicholas Darvas and Jesse Livermore, were predominantly price-action trend followers. In his book 'How I Made $2 Million in the Stock Market' Darvas cautions that even if you don't like the trend, it's no use trying to fight it. In Edwin Lefevre's book 'Reminiscences of a Stock Operator' the fictional character Larry Livingston – who we presume to be Jesse Livermore – suggests that in a bull market the game is to buy and hold until you think that the bull market is near its end.

Don't be alarmed by the phrase 'buy and hold' in that quote. What he's saying is that it is ok to buy and hold... until the trend changes.

Having studied those books, and many others, my conclusions are as follows:

Don't Lose Money (in the Stock Markets)

1. It might not matter exactly when you enter a rising market, as long as you're prepared to get out quickly if you're wrong.

2. You should ride the uptrend as long as possible, until the trend breaks.

Both 1 and 2 help should ensure you don't lose money (which is most important), and 2 should ensure you make as much as possible.

Purists would point out that in the days before ETFs existed, Livermore was talking about trading individual stocks. That may be true, but his trades were always in the context of the behavior of the overall market as represented by the Dow Jones industrial Average. Indeed, he hinted that if he could buy the whole market, he would.

Timing and Trend Following in Practice
Although I stated above that "it might not matter when you enter a rising market", I find it quite demoralizing if the tide turns quickly and I have to sell out at a loss. So I try to buy in at a time when I think that the balance of probabilities is in favor of a rise, at least in the short term.

Figure 4 shows a typical bull market 'saw tooth' graph characterized by gradual upward price movements punctuated by sudden downturns. I've annotated that graph with my ideal BUY and DON'T BUY points.

It is clear that buying at the BUY points would result in an immediate profit, whereas buying at the DON'T BUY points would result in an immediate loss.

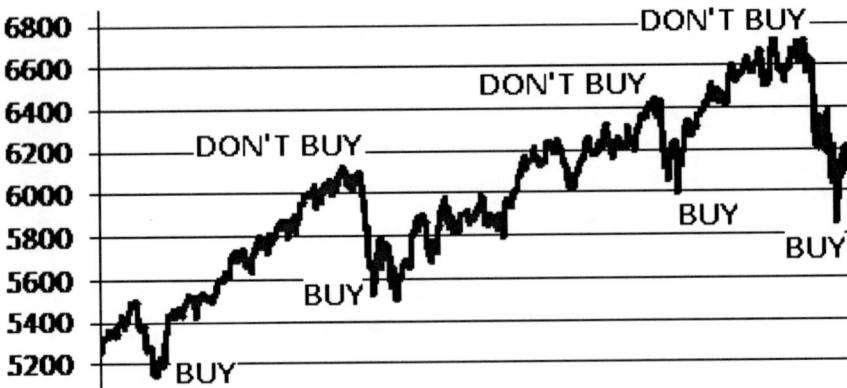

Figure 4 Bull Market Saw Tooth Graph

Even if I didn't buy on the dips I'd be buying into a general upward trend, but the psychological pressure to sell out after an immediate – albeit temporary – loss would be too much to bear; especially as my overriding motivation is to <u>not lose money</u>. Just as it should be, as we never really know when the trend will truly break.

At this point you might be reading too much into my DON'T BUY points, interpreting them as SELL points. Well they might be, and they might not, as I'll discuss in the next chapter. Remember that the aim is to ride the trend as long as possible until you're sure it's the end of the trend.

Jesse Livermore recounted that disregarding the big swing and trying to jump in and out was fatal to him; and pointed out that nobody can catch all the fluctuations.

Are you wondering how I decided on the BUY and DON'T BUY points in Figure 4? I didn't use moving averages or any other advanced 'technical indicators'. For the BUY points I simply look for major downward market corrections, which are easy to spot and possible to benefit from retrospectively because markets usually rise slower than they fall (hence the saw tooth shape). I showed DON'T BUY points merely for illustration; in practice I don't really look for them at all because they require no action!

Experience Note

Figure 4 makes it look easy; just buy on the dips. Not just any dips; the significant corrections. But in practice catching the bottom of the correction is not always straightforward, as I know all too well.

A recent example springs to mind, as demonstrated by Figure 5.

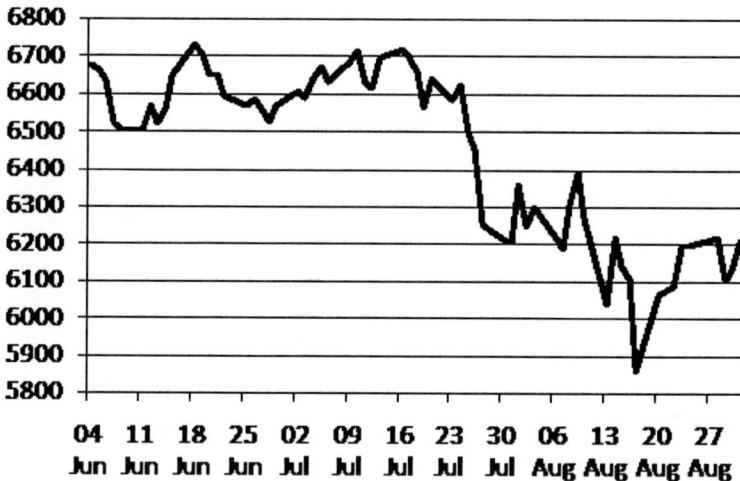

Figure 5 FTSE 100, 4 June - 31 August 2007

On 23 July 2007 the correction began and the value of the FTSE index dropped noticeably. Past experience taught me not to buy-in straightaway because such a notable, newsworthy, fall is usually followed by further falls over two or three days. Around the third day I bought the index, which at the time was the right decision because the index subsequently rose.

On 31 July it fell, so I sold out; Around 5 August it rose again so I bought back in, and around 7 August it fell so I sold out. That pattern repeated as I tried to find the bottom of the correction.

My post mortem of the trades up to that point can be summarized as follows:

- I avoided incurring any single big loss, including the one that would have resulted from the fall between 11 and 17 August.

- I incurred several small losses stemming from not timing the trades perfectly, from the difference between the buying and selling prices (the bid-ask spread), and from the stockbroker's transaction charge on each trade. I'll say more about bid-ask spreads and transaction charges in Chapter 4.

The end result was that the balance of my trading account fell between 23 July and 17 August so, yes, I lost money. But not as much as I would have lost if I had bought in on the first day of the correction and held on all the way down.

Such losses are inevitable when trying to time the entry into a highly volatile market; but I tried to limit the losses by trading an index ETF with a very small bid-ask spread (they're not all the same), by using a stockbroker offering low transaction charges, and by setting tight stops (see next chapter) to sell out at the slightest sign of trouble.

The see-saw pattern repeated until 31 August when my tactics changed. As you can imagine, I last bought in on the low point around 26 August, so by 31 August the trade was in profit. At that point I concluded that the correction might be complete, so I widened my stop (again, see next chapter) to allow greater tolerance of temporary price falls.

Don't Lose Money (in the Stock Markets)

Why did 31 August signal an end of the correction to me? Because at that point a pattern was establishing whereby each price peak was higher than the one before, and each price trough was higher than the one before. Prices were now trending upwards, and I would ride the new uptrend as far as I could without selling out.

If you're wondering what happened after 31 August I can tell you that the index did continue its general uptrend, but it was a rocky road; just as rocky as the road down, with many threats of a trend reversal. So while I felt justified in widening my stops, I was wise not to do away with them entirely.

If I subsequently turned out to be totally wrong in my assessment, and correction turned to crash, I'd avoid the worst.

What's the Alternative?

The alternative to market timing and trend following, which are technical in nature, is to invest based on company fundamentals. I've tried that too, and found it to not suit my trading style.

The problem I faced is that while an individual stock might be underpriced compared with its true value (however you measure that), it can take a long time for that true value to be reflected in the price. In the mean time you may have to hold on to a stock that is going nowhere; or even falling in the short term. In other words, you need enough faith to accept a short term loss in the hope of a possible long term gain. That's not ideal if your aim is to not lose money.

On the other hand, if you're investing in indexes – as I do – then an appreciation of 'market' fundamentals may be beneficial. When deciding on market timing entries and exits

I try to keep in mind the general market conditions at the time. Is the whole market bullish or bearish? Are we experiencing a classic bubble that might burst at any time? Are interest rates and inflation historically high or low?

The 'market' fundamentals may give an insight as to <u>where</u> the market will go, up or down, but not necessarily <u>when</u>. The top of a speculative bubble might be good time to think about going into cash, or trading short, but not until the price action confirms that the bubble really is bursting.

Don't Lose Money!
Time the Market, Follow the trend.

Chapter 3 – Use Stops

The majority of the (good) trading books I've read give the following advice:

"Cut your losses and let your profits run"

This is contrary to the instincts of many naïve traders who hold on to losing trades ("because they will surely recover") and get out of profitable trades ("because no-one goes broke by taking a profit").

The problem is that you could hold a losing position all the way down to zero, all the while tying up your money that could be better invested elsewhere. And on the other side, by selling out too soon you will miss the maximum potential of each trade.

Think about trading as a business, like a high street clothing business. If the red dress is generating healthy profits and the green dress is not selling at all, you invest more in stocks of red dresses and offer green dresses for quick sale.

If you accept that argument, you'll need a mechanism for cutting losses and letting profits run. That mechanism is the stop-loss order, or simply the 'stop'.

Mental Stops

A 'stop' is a price at which you will sell out (cut your losses) if a price falls to a predetermined level or by a predetermined amount. If you buy into the S&P index at

1500 you might decide to close the trade if the price falls to 1485; a fall of 15 points, or 1%.

Yes I know this book is about not losing money, but accepting a 1% loss may well save you from a 10% loss.

I call this a 'mental stop' because you would have the stop price in the back of your mind while you monitor the price movements. All well and good if you are in a position to continually monitor the price, and if you're disciplined enough to actually press the SELL button when the stop price is reached. Most people aren't.

Stop Orders

Most stockbrokers will allow you to place 'stop orders' on-line or by telephone at no extra charge. This puts the onus on the stockbroker to monitor the price for you and sell out automatically when the stop is breached. Meantime you can get on with your life.

All of my trading accounts (regular trading, ISA, and SIPP) provide a stop order facility, as does my spread trading account. In fact my 'limited risk' spread trading account attaches a stop order automatically to any trade I make.

Trailing Stops

Some, but not all, stockbrokers provide an enhanced form of stop order called a 'trailing stop order'. The idea being that as the price rises, so does the stop point.

For example:

If the S&P index rose from 1500 to 1515, your stop point would automatically be raised from 1485 to 1500. Which means from that time onwards your trade will never close at a loss. And if the S&P then rose to 1525, your stop point would rise to 1510 giving a guaranteed profit of 10 points. All the while your profits can run providing the price never falls by 15 points from its last peak.

I chose a 15-point stop merely for illustration. It can be whatever you like, but I do make some recommendations shortly.

My three stockbroker trading accounts allow for trailing stop orders attached to specific stocks, and to indexes traded in the form of Exchange Traded Funds (ETFs). My spread trading account provides stop orders but not trailing stops, but there's nothing to prevent me from trailing those stops myself by raising the stop price periodically; which I do.

Guaranteed Stops

I used the word 'guaranteed' somewhat liberally in the previous section. In most cases stop orders are not guaranteed, and merely promise to sell out at-or-below the stop price. Most times this won't matter, but beware that on occasions the stop price that you achieve may be less than what you expect if:

- There has been some slippage between the time that the stop order is triggered and the time that it is actually dealt.

- The market has 'gapped', meaning that the price has moved notably in out-of-hours trading between the close of the market yesterday and the open of the market today.

You might just have to live with the fact that a non-guaranteed stop is better than no stop at all. However, in some cases there is something you can do about it.

My stockbroker allows a 'limit' to be set for each stop order. So I can specify, for example, that I want to sell out if the S&P index falls to 1485 or less but not if the price has gapped below 1450. Beware that with such a stop-limit order I run the risk of not selling out at all.

My spread trading provider does allow, and in fact insists on, a guaranteed stop on my 'limited risk' account for every trade I place. Any bet I make on the FTSE is guaranteed to stop out at 40 points below my opening price. Any bet I make on the Dow Jones is guaranteed to stop out at 70 points below my opening price. Even if the market gaps 100 points down in either case, the 40-point or 70-point guaranteed stops will be honored. It's not charity though, as a small commission is charged for that guarantee.

Sell Stops vs. Buy Stops
In my coverage of stops above I've been talking only about 'sell stops'; those that get you out of a trade at – or near – a specified price.

In fact there is a complementary type of stop on the buying side, a 'buy stop'; the idea here being to buy a stock or index when its prices rises to a particular level. This might be useful if the market has suffered a correction (say 10% down) from 1500 to 1350 and you wish to buy in if it starts to rise again past 1400. That is, you want to buy in if the price action confirms a resumption of the up-trend.

Since buy stops do not constitute a capital protection mechanism I won't consider them further in this book.

How tight to set those stops
One of the biggest problems, when using sell stops, is how tight to set them.

Don't Lose Money (in the Stock Markets)

On the one hand, very tight stops will limit the loss on any one trade to a very small amount. But they will be triggered frequently; which means more work for you and more commissions for the stockbroker as you establish new positions.

On the other hand, wide stops will be triggered seldom but you will lose more money on each trade that stops out.

My own preference is to set tight stops on the way down while I'm trying to find the bottom of a market correction, in order to cut my potential losses short; and to set them wide on the way up, to let my profits run.

In the market conditions shown in Figure 6 I would set tight stops during the period 23 July to 17 August, and wide stops from 26 August onwards. In the intervening time 18 August to 25 August I would keep stops tight to make sure that a new uptrend has established before I widen those stops.

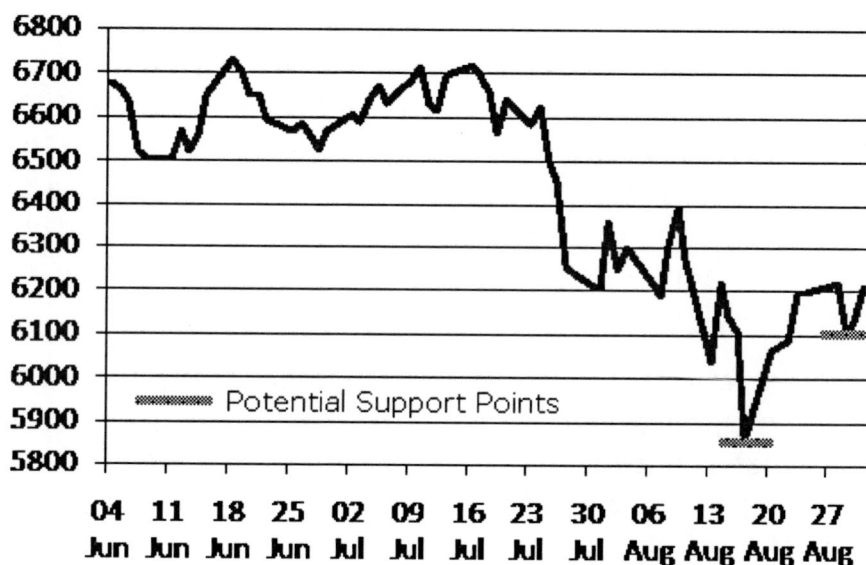

Figure 6 FTSE 100, 4 June - 31 August 2007, with Support Points

So what do I mean by a tight stop, and what do I mean by a wide stop?

How tight is tight, how wide is wide?

The first thing to bear in mind is the noise, or general variation in prices during the trading day; whereby a price may fall, then rise, then fall by a small amount during the day for no apparent reason. Typically for a major index there might be up to 1% variation in price during the day simply due to this 'noise'.

Usually it makes little sense to set a stop at less than 1% below the current price unless you want to get stopped out for no reason. So in my opinion, a tight stop would be anywhere from 1% below the current price up to about 2% below the current price. I don't want to lose more than 2% on any one trade if I make a wrong call in a down trending market. Remember, don't lose money.

In an upward trending market – and the best confirmation of that is if my last trade is in profit – I will widen my stop initially to about 2.5% below the current price. I say 'initially' because in an upward trending market my aim is to keep the stops as wide as possible, as long as I would stop out at a profit. So once my trade is in profit by a healthy 10% I might be happy to have a 5% stop-point, thus capturing at least half the profit if the tide turns.

Something else to consider is whether there are any apparent support points in the price chart. In Figure 6 you can see that the lowest price reached was around 5860, at which point market traders stopped selling and starting buying. The price subsequently rose to 6200, inevitably fell back a little (to 6100) and then started rising again. That suggests two possible support points, at 5860 and 6100, which marked the turning points between net selling and net buying.

Investopedia (www.investopedia.com) defines a 'support point' or 'support level' as "The price level which, historically, a stock has had difficulty falling below. It is thought of as the level at which a lot of buyers tend to enter the stock."

So rather than setting stops at a percentage below the current price, how about setting stops to coincide with those support points? As each new support point becomes apparent, raise your stop to that new level. Some traders do just that.

In using stops, and trailing them upwards, I am in good company. One of the greatest traders of all time, Nicholas Darvas, expressed his approach to stop orders in his book 'How I Made $2 Million in the Stock Market'. That approach was:

- To hold on to a rising stock but, at the same time, keep raising the stop-loss order parallel with its rise.

- To keep [the stop-loss order] at such a distance that a meaningless swing in price would not touch it off.

Experience Note
In the period 23 July to 17 August I used very tight stops and got stopped out several times at a small loss while trying to find the bottom of the correction.

On the way back up I used trailing stops on my regular trading, ISA, and SIPP stockbroker accounts, which by their nature required me to set a percentage stop level; e.g. stop out if the price falls by 2.5% from any peak.

On the way back up I used non-trailing stops on my spread trading account, simply because that account does not provide them. Since I was responsible for adjusting those stops myself, I adjusted them upwards each time a new support point was established. The width of those stops was determined, therefore, not by a set percentage, but by the distance between the current price and the last support point.

The Price Ratchet

I think of stop orders as a kind of 'price ratchet' that can turn only one way. When the price rises, the ratchet turns; when the price falls, the ratchet stops.

Don't Lose Money!
Use Stops.

Chapter 4 – Keep Trading Costs Low

In this chapter the aim is to look at how you can avoid losing money by keeping your trading costs low. I don't mean the costs associated with making bad trading decisions (buying in to loss-making stocks or indexes), but those costs that are incurred regardless of whether trades go well or badly.

Bid-Ask Spread

All trades are subject to a bid-ask spread; the difference between the buying price and selling price of a security (whether an individual stock or an index ETF). Your stockbroker will quote one price at which he's willing to sell to you (the ask price), and another – lower – price at which he's willing to buy back from you (the bid price). Just like when you buy and sell foreign currency at the bureau-de-change.

On very liquid frequently-traded stocks such as blue chip companies, and on popular ETFs, the spread tends to be quite small. On less liquid thinly-traded stocks such as smaller companies, and on less popular ETFs, the spread can be quite wide.

Today my stockbroker is offering the following buying and selling prices on two different stocks:

Vodafone Group: sell @ 160.60, buy @ 160.70

Tadpole Technology: sell @ 4, buy @ 5

That means that if I bought Vodafone and wanted to sell out straightaway I would lose just 0.06% of my stake whereas if I bought Tadpole and wanted to sellout straightaway I would lose a whopping 20% of my stake. Or to put it another way, my Tadpole shares would have to rise by an impressive 25% before I even got my original stake back.

As I've already explained, I prefer to trade index ETFs rather than specific stocks. Again, there is some variation in spreads between different ETFs as the following samples taken today show:

'IShares S&P 500 NAV' ETF: sell @ 727.5, buy @ 728.5 (0.14%)

'IShares FTSE 250 Fund' ETF: sell @ 1117, buy @ 1120.5 (0.31%)

'IShares MSCI Japan Fund' ETF: sell @ 686, buy @ 689 (0.44%)

'IShares FTSE/XINHUA CHINA 25 NAV' ETF: sell @ 6993, buy @ 7058 (0.92%)

If you bought into the S&P 500 index ETF at 728.5 you would be down 0.14% immediately, and if you bought into the CHINA 25 ETF you would be down 0.92% immediately. If you trade frequently it goes without saying that the narrower the spreads, the less you'll lose.

Regular trading accounts and spread trading accounts (the clue is in the name) are both subject to bid-ask spreads. Whereas on spread trading accounts that is the only direct cost to bear, on regular trading accounts there will be an additional transaction charge for each trade.

Don't Lose Money (in the Stock Markets)

Transaction Charges

Yes, my spread trading provider takes his cut solely from the difference between his buying and selling prices. Except that I'm running a 'limited risk' account with mandatory guaranteed stop losses; which means an additional £6 ($12) on each trade to guarantee the stop.

My regular stockbroker passes the cut from the bid-ask spread directly to the market maker who executes the trades. So the stockbroker's cut has to come from somewhere else – the 'transaction charge' or 'dealing charge'. This fee can vary according to which stockbroker you use, whether you deal by telephone or internet, and how often you trade.

Currently my stockbroker charges around £6.95 (about $14) per online trade providing I trade more than 10 times per quarter. If I traded less frequently, by telephone, the fee would be £12.50 or more per trade. Needless to say, I trade online to cut costs.

Other Management Charges

My regular trading account has no additional fees, but my tax-friendly ISA and SIPP accounts are also subject to an annual 'management fee' which is unavoidable. This fee is based on the value of my portfolio, up to a limit.

Currently it goes something like this:

- £20 for a portfolio value up to £50,000.

- £40 for a portfolio value over £50,000.

Therefore the percentage fee on a £1,000 holding would be 2%, and on an £49,999 it would be 0.04%. For a £50,001 holding the fee would rise slightly to 0.08%, reducing thereafter.

For some time I kept my portfolio just below £50,000 so as to benefit from the lower fee. Now that my portfolio is above £50,000 I intend to grow it as big as I can, so that the fee becomes progressively lower as a proportion.

Tax

As the saying goes, there are only two things certain in life – death and taxes. I can think of three kinds of taxes associated with share trading, which all go to the government:

- Stamp Duty which (at least in the UK) is levied whenever you purchase shares. Currently 0.5% of the value traded.

- Income Tax which is levied on any dividends you receive from your stock holdings.

- Capital Gains Tax which is levied when you sell shares based on any increase in value since you bought them.

I'm not a qualified tax adviser, so I won't be giving any direct advice. But I can tell you that in the UK under current tax legislation:

- ISA and SIPP accounts are free from income tax and capital gains tax; although equity ISAs do suffer a 10% tax-at-source on dividends, which cannot be reclaimed.

- Regular trading accounts suffer income and capital gains taxes, but you can offset your personal annual allowances and – depending how long you hold the assets within them – claim capital gains taper relief.

- Stamp duty is levied on individual stocks, but currently not on ETFs. Another reason why I like them.

- Spread Trading (aka spread betting) in the UK is currently free from all the aforementioned taxes because – technically – it's not investing, it's gambling. As there are more gambling losers than winners, the government would make a net loss by making gambling taxable – hence tax-deductible!

US citizens could save on tax by taking advantage of the 401(k) retirement plan, the Individual Retirement Account (IRA), or – in some cases – the 529 College Savings Plan.

For completeness I'll also mention 'withholding tax' which may be levied by a government on foreign investors. An ETF may itself be subjected to withholding tax; for example if an ETF provided by the Ireland-based iShares invests in the (US) Dow Jones. A private UK individual would be subjected to US withholding tax if he invested in Dow Jones or NASDAQ stocks through a US broker. The withholding tax may be avoided by filing the US Internal Revenue Service (IRS) form W-8BEN, but you would still have to pay UK income tax on the income received.

You might be interested to know that as an author I am subjected to withholding tax (at 30%) on book royalties from my US publishers; unless, of course, I complete the form W-8BEN.

Experience Note
My direct trading costs used to be far too high.

As a naïve trader, on more than one occasion I bought shares in an individual stock that had a wide bid-ask spread. No doubt based on a 'tip' that this small company was about to rocket.

For the sake of argument, let's assume it was Tadpole Technology; and I choose that stock not because it was the real one involved in that case (Baltimore Technologies, I think), but because the similar unfavorable bid-ask spread illustrates my point.

As soon as my investment of £10,000 had been accepted my holding would be worth:

£10,000 (initial investment) * 0.8 (the bid-ask spread) = £8,000 minus 0.5% (of £10,000; the stamp duty) = £7,950.

That stock really would have to rocket, by almost 26% just to recover my original stake.

These days I'm much more likely to buy the S&P 500 index ETF, with its narrow bid-ask spread and no stamp duty. Thus my £10,000 investment would reduce by only £14 initially, which I regard as negligible.

Both then and now I would suffer the additional £6.95 transaction fee, but at least I've reduced that fee by trading on-line rather than by telephone.

Providing I trade via my ISA or SIPP account, there will be no additional income- or capital gains- taxes to pay no matter how much profit I make on the trade. And providing the profits on my regular trading account are less than my annual capital gains allowance (currently £9,200) I'll be relatively tax efficient there too.

Who says that only the mega-rich can avoid tax? And it gets better.

As my spread trading activities are totally tax free no matter how much profit I make, and with narrow spreads such as 13319 – 13325 on the Dow Jones, I could be laughing all the way to the bank!

Don't Lose Money (in the Stock Markets)

I say 'could' because obviously there's the small matter of my trades actually being profitable trades.

As for my losing trades: I'll stop out of those quite quickly if they go the wrong way. And that's where keeping trading costs low really counts; because the more you stop out, the more you trade. The more you trade, the more you pay by way of bid-ask spreads, transaction fees, and stamp duty.

Don't Lose Money!
Keep Trading Costs Low.

Don't Lose Money (in the Stock Markets)

Chapter 5 – Size Your Positions

In his book 'Trade Your Way to Financial Freedom' Van K Tharp suggests that, historically, the coverage of position sizing has been inadequate, noting that most books on trading systems simply do not cover the subject.

He endeavors to put that right, and so will I.

My book is predominantly about money management, which means trying not to incur losses. Position sizing is an aspect of money management just as important as, and complementary to, the other money management techniques – such as stop losses – that I've already discussed.

Definition of Position Sizing

There is perhaps no single agreed definition of 'position sizing', but it will be helpful in my discussions for you to understand my definition to be:

The amount of money you commit to a trade initially, and maintain throughout the life of a trade; as a proportion of your available funds.

So it's not just the amount you commit initially in setting up a position, but also the amount(s) by which you alter that position over time as your confidence in the position grows and shrinks. And all the while remembering that this is relative to the funds you have available, since the overriding goal when trading should always be to 'stay in the game'. There's no point committing 100% of your available funds to a single dodgy trade that wipes you out.

He who trades and runs away lives to trade another day; and the longer you stay in the game, the greater your chance of catching the big wave.

Initial Position Size

How much you commit to a trade initially may depend on a number of factors including: your expectation of the trade's potential, and your confidence that your expectation will be realized.

In Figure 7 I once again chart the course of the FTSE 100 index between 4 June and 31 August 2007, this time with an indication of 'expectation' and 'confidence' levels at two strategic points.

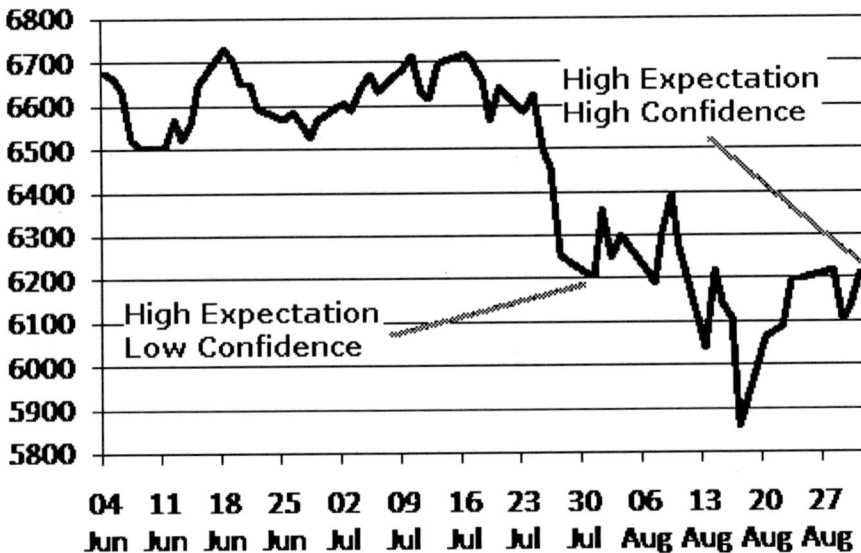

Figure 7 FTSE 100, 4 June - 31 August 2007, with Expectation and Confidence

At both of the points indicated the index stands at 6200 yet the expectation and confidence profiles are different.

Don't Lose Money (in the Stock Markets)

At the first point, around 29 July, you might have high expectations. If the correction has completed, a subsequent rebound back up to the previous high of 6700 would yield 8%. But you can't be sure that the correction has completed, so you might establish a relatively small position to test the bottom.

At the second point, around 29 August, your expectations would be equally high. But this time you might be more confident in those expectations being realized, because an up-trend has been established and you have witnessed two support points – at around 5900 and 6100 respectively. So in that case you might establish a much larger position.

This raises the question of what do I consider to be a large initial position and a small initial position.

In his book 'The Zurich Axioms' Max Gunther advises to "play for meaningful stakes" on the basis that even if you double your money on a $100 stake, you're still poor. I recall reading a similar sentiment in one of George Soros's books prefixed with the words "If you're confident that you're right…"

The implication is that if the odds are stacked in your favor you might as well commit as much as you can; 100% of your available funds. If you're wrong your stop loss order (remember?) will help to protect you.

At this point you might be thinking "Why don't I commit 100% of available funds even when I'm not so confident? After all, the stop loss order will protect me."

To answer that question we need to look at the interplay between position sizes and stops.

Position Sizes and Stops

A popular trading maxim is that you should only trade what you can afford to lose.

Let's suppose you're willing to lose no more than $100 on any one trade, and your available funds are $10,000. You can limit your loss to $100 in two different ways:

1. Commit the full $10,000 and set a stop at 1% below the trade price.

2. Commit $2,500 and set a stop at 4% below the trade price.

Option 1 will generate bigger profits if the price rises, but you're more likely to get stopped out if the price falls. That means you'll trade more often, each time racking up transaction costs.

Option 2 will not be so profitable but will be more tolerant of market noise.

Also consider that if you had $100,000 of available funds you would need to set a stop at minus 0.1% in order to limit your losses to $100 per trade. You would surely get stopped out frequently at that level, so perhaps with a personal fortune of $100,000 it's time consider raising your allowable loss-per-trade!

Ongoing Position Sizing

Having said that Option 2 above would not be as profitable as Option 1, there is something you can do to improve the situation. You could commit more funds as your initial $2,500 investment rises.

Suppose you make the initial investment at an index level of 6,200. If the index falls, you sell out at a loss of $100. If the index rises to 6,400, your investment grows by 3.22% to $2,580.

Now suppose that the index recovers all the way back to its previous high of 6,700. Your investment will have grown by 8% to $2,700. That's a nice return in a short time but the $200 increase represents only a 2% rise on your total $10,000 available funds.

What if you had increased the size of your position by investing an additional $2,500 when the index has risen from 6,200 to 6,400? Once the index had fully recovered, your original investment would be worth $2,700 as before, and your second investment would be worth about $2,617. Thus your combined investments would have risen by 6.3%; and your total funds by 3.17%.

You should now see where I'm going with this. If you invested a further $2,500 at 6,500 and the same at 6,600, thus exhausting you $10,000 available funds, you total return would be:

- $2,500 invested at 6,200 becomes $2,700

- $2,500 invested at 6,400 becomes $2,617

- $2,500 invested at 6,500 becomes $2,577

- $2,500 invested at 6,600 becomes $2,538

Thus the total investment (over time) of $10,000 has become $10,432; a 4.32% profit. That's more than double the profit achieved by maintaining the original position at $2,500.

Once in Profit, Stay in Profit

We could do even better by adding the whole remaining available funds ($7,500) to the original position once the index has risen from 6,200 to 6,400; but here's the problem.

By doubling the position size from $2,500 to $5,000 at the 6400 level we effectively halved the profit showing at that point from 3.22% to 1.61%.

Alternatively, by investing the remaining funds of $7,500 at 6,400 we would reduce the percentage profit showing at that point to 0.8%. Our absolute paper profit in cash terms has not changed since 1.61% of $5,000 is the same as 0.8% of $10,000, but the fall in the percentage profit is important as follows.

What if the index itself fell 1% and we had a stop loss order set at -1%? In the first case (of less aggressive position sizing), the stop order would trigger and we would make a net profit of 1.61% minus 1% = 0.61% (of $5,000 = $30.50 profit). In the second case (more aggressive position sizing), the stop order would trigger and we would actually make a loss of 0.8% minus 1% = -0.2% (of $10,000 = $20 loss).

Remember, don't lose money!

In fact, not losing money gets easier as you make further contributions. Whereas the first same-amount top-up reduces the apparent profit by half:

- The second same-amount top-up preserves two-thirds of the accrued profit; e.g. an apparent profit of 3.22% on a $5,000 investment falls only to 2.15% (not 1.61%) upon making an additional $2,500 investment.

- The third same-amount top-up preserves 75% of the accrued profit; e.g. an apparent profit of 3.22% on a

$7,500 investment falls to only 2.42% (not 1.61%, nor 2.15%) upon making an additional $2,500 investment.

Pyramiding

What I've been describing is a form of pyramiding, which is a well-known technique for making additional investments in a stock or index that is rising.

Another form of pyramiding would be to reinvest the dividends that you receive as cash from you holdings. Some investment vehicles provide automatic reinvestment of dividends, but I prefer to take the decision voluntarily each time a dividend is paid. The reason is simple: I only want to reinvest dividends in risers, not fallers.

Pyramiding using dividend payments may be advantageous if you have already committed all of your available funds, and obviously not advantageous if you need the regular income that dividends provide.

You might also be wondering how this might apply to indexes as well as to stocks. Well, I can tell you that the index ETFs I mention do all pay dividends – in proportion to the dividends paid by the individual stocks comprising those indexes.

Experience Note

My family's basic household running costs – no luxuries – amount to something like £2,000 ($4,000) per month. So as a bare minimum I need to generate £100 ($200) per trading day in order to stay afloat.

In the absence of any other advantage, by sheer chance half of my trades will be profitable and half won't. I reckon I <u>can</u> make a net £100 per day (else I wouldn't be doing this) so at a 50/50 success-fail ratio I need to make £100 for every £0 that I lose, or £200 for every £100 that I lose, or £300 for every £200 that I lose... and so on.

My acceptable average loss per day is therefore £100, and since I intend to trade once <u>per day</u> I've set my acceptable loss <u>per trade</u> at £100. As I don't want to get stopped out every day simply due to noise, I'd like to set my stops at minus 2%.

My optimal initial position size therefore works out at £5,000, because 2% of £5,000 is the £100 that I'm willing to lose.

On the downward leg of Figure 7, 23 July - 16 August, while my expectation was high but confidence low, that position size limited my potential loss per day to an acceptable level.

On the upward leg, 17 August onwards, I committed an additional £5,000 once my initial investment showed a profit of around 5%. At that point the doubling up of my investment reduced the apparent profit to 2.5%, and since my stop loss is set at minus 2% I stood to get out with at least 0.5% profit in any event.

Don't Lose Money!
Size Your Positions.

Chapter 6 – Use Straddles and Strangles

In the preceding chapters I've talked mainly about strategies for limiting your losses when trading the market long; i.e. when speculating that prices will rise.

Your stockbroker might let you speculate the other way – that prices will fall – by allowing you to sell shares that you don't actually own in the hope of buying them back in future at a lower price. Even if your stockbroker won't let you do this, you might be able to trade short using derivatives such as 'options'.

Both my regular trading account and my SIPP account allow me to trade 'covered warrants' (a form of options) and 'listed contracts for difference' (similar to options). In fact I must use these derivative tradable instruments if I wish to trade indexes short, because I can't do that via ETFs.

Let me say up-front that I'm not necessarily suggesting that you trade options, which can be more risky than ETFs and other non-leveraged securities. What I'm suggesting is that if you must trade options – because it's the only way you can trade both long and short – then it's safer to do so using straddles and strangles.

The Long and Short of Options
The two things you really need to know about options is that they have:

- A Strike Price above which (when trading long) or below which (when trading short) the trade pays off.

- An Expiry Date at which, or by which, your trade must be profitable.

To trade options long you buy a CALL, and to trade options short you buy a PUT.

Suppose your stockbroker offers you a Dow Jones CALL with strike price 14000 and expiry date 31 March 2008. If the index stands above strike price 14000 on the expiry date your trade will pay off, otherwise it won't. That is shown graphically in Figure 8.

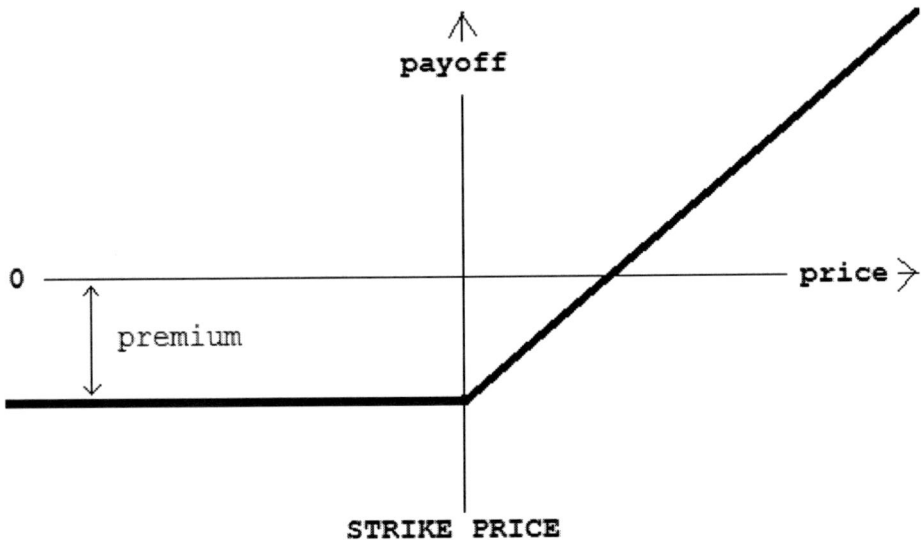

Figure 8 Payoff for a CALL option at the strike date

Ok, so I didn't tell the whole truth in the previous paragraph. As you can see in Figure 8, you need the index value to rise slightly higher than the strike price for your CALL option to pay off. That's because you've paid a premium to take the option in the first place, and a payoff comes only when the rising price exceeds the premium.

Your maximum loss, indicated by the horizontal portion of the payoff line, would be limited to the premium you paid.

Your maximum payoff would be proportional to how far the index had risen above the strike price by the strike date.

The payoff graph for a PUT option is the exact mirror, as shown in Figure 9. In that case your option would pay off on the strike date if the price has fallen to less than the strike price plus premium paid. Your trade would not pay off if the index price were to be higher than the strike price on the strike date.

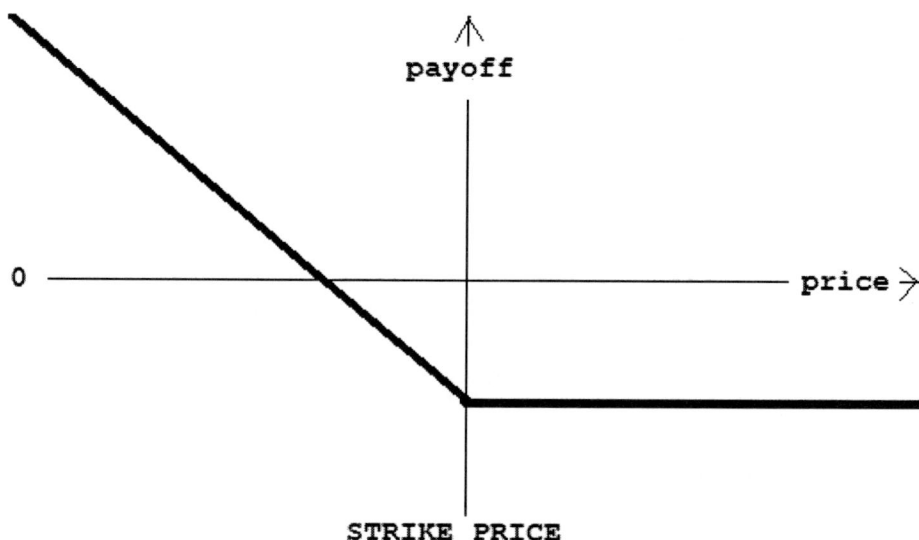

Figure 9 Payoff for a PUT option at the strike date

Note that in both cases there is unlimited upside potential and limited downside potential. Although the downside is limited, that limitation is still equal to the premium you paid. That doesn't sound too promising in our quest to avoid losing money, does it?

Straddles and Strangles

Imagine that you could simultaneously buy CALL and PUT options, both at the same strike price and strike date. The effect would be that, as the value of one option fell, the value of the other would rise to compensate. On the face of it you can't lose, and you can't win either.

Actually, you can lose a little but your loss is limited to the two premiums paid to take out the options. And actually you can win too, because the upside on the winning option is unlimited whereas the downside on the losing option is limited to your initial stake. This can be illustrated by merging the previous two figures into Figure 10.

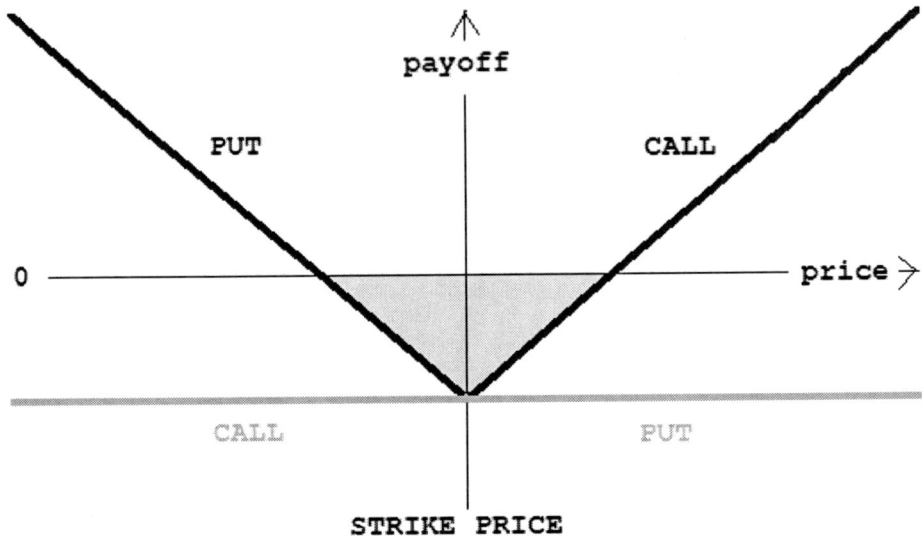

Figure 10 Option Straddle

In that figure you can see that as long as the index price has exceeded the strike price + premiums paid, there is nothing more to lose on the PUT option and everything to gain on the CALL option. Providing the index has fallen to less than the strike price - premiums paid, there is nothing more to lose on the CALL option and everything to gain on the PUT option.

With an 'option straddle' therefore you gain whichever way the price goes, as long as it does not land within the range (strike price – premiums paid) to (strike price + premiums paid) on the expiry date.

Don't Lose Money (in the Stock Markets)

Most importantly you've protected yourself from losing money if you 'bet the wrong way'.

In reality you may find it difficult to establish an option spread – which is what a straddle is – with both legs (CALL and PUT) having the same strike price. For example: today my stockbroker is offering a CALL covered warrant on the Dow Jones at strike price 14000, and a PUT with the same expiry date at strike price 12000.

During a period of high volatility, such as we're in as I write this, I might consider it still to be a good play; because I'm expecting the index to move a large amount before the expiry date, but I don't know which way. The effect of the different strike prices is as shown in Figure 11.

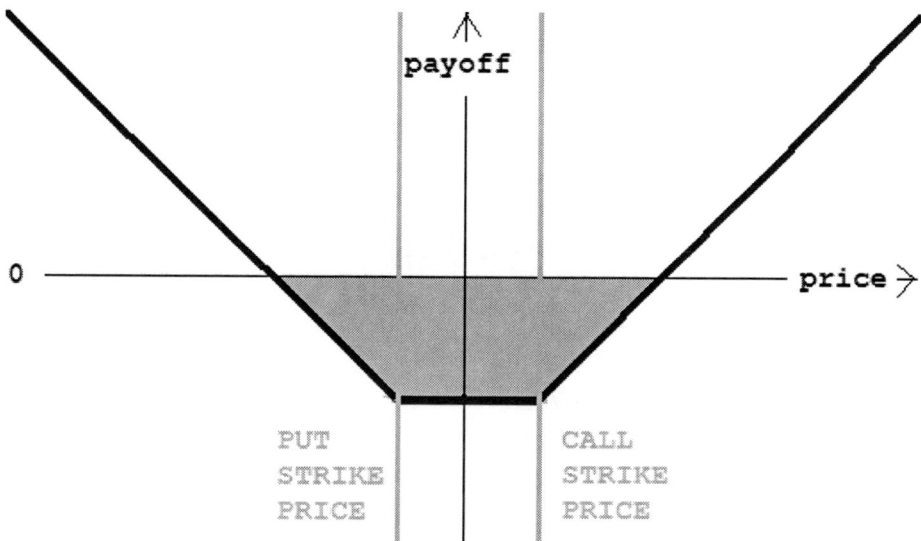

Figure 11 Option Strangle

The area of potential loss (shaded) has been extended to accommodate the two different strike prices.

The implication of this is obvious. To limit your losses when establishing a 'strangle' you should aim for the strike prices on the CALL and PUT legs of the spread to be as close together as possible; i.e. as close to a straddle as you can get.

Other Option Spreads

Straddles and strangles, as described above, represent the two most common option spreads. There are other kinds – with exotic names like 'costless collar' and 'butterfly' – that are beyond this scope of this book. Those spreads are established by taking options with different strike prices and different expiry dates.

I'm happy to stick with the advice given by Guy Cohen in his book 'Options Made Easy'. That is, choose options having the same expiry date and with strike prices equidistant from the current market price.

Exercising Options

Theoretically, when you buy an option you're buying the right – but not the obligation – to buy or sell the underlying asset (e.g. an individual stock) at the given strike price on the expiry date.

Most times, traders exercise options prior to expiry thereby never actually taking ownership of an underlying asset; and in the case of index options there is no underlying asset as such, so these are 'cash settled' at any time up to the expiry date. Which means the stockbroker simply pays out your net gain or loss at the time you cash in.

Since you can cash in at any time – for European-style options anyway – it makes sense to do this when the gain on one leg of the spread exceeds the loss on the other leg by a meaningful amount. So once your $1,000 investment in the CALL leg has risen to $3,000, and at the same time your

$1,000 investment in the PUT leg has fallen to an insignificant amount (never quite zero until the expiry date), it might be time to bank the $3,000 which includes a net $1,000 (50%) gain. Wait any longer and it might slip away.

A more advanced strategy would be to cash in only the CALL option, in the hope that sometime before the expiry date the index might fall substantially thus rendering the PUT option once again worth something.

Experience Note

Most non-professional traders do not have the luxury of taking options that meet an exact specification of expiry date and strike price. You are limited to the range of options offered by financial institutions via your stockbroker.

So to find two opposing options (CALL and PUT) with strike prices equidistant from the current market price, and having an expiry date sufficiently in the future to give time for success, is something of a tall order.

For me, such an ideal set-up occurred around 29 July 2007. On that day my stockbroker was offering a CALL option on the FTSE 100 at strike price 6400 and a PUT option at 6000. Both options had an expiry date of 19 December 2008, plenty of time to come good, and the current market price was 6200.

I bought in to both options to establish a 'strangle', safe in the knowledge that I could never lose more than my combined investment of £5,000 (£2,500 on each leg); and only then if the value of the index happens to sit between 6000 and 6400 on the expiry date. Between now and then there would be plenty of time for my gamble to pay off.

You'll be wondering why I'm comfortable with a potential £5,000 loss, however unlikely I think that is. After all, I don't want to lose money.

Well there's something I omitted to mention in my coverage of options; the small matter of 'leverage'. As a leveraged instrument, the value of an option rises or falls at a greater rate than the underlying index. So if my CALL option is leveraged 10:1 then a 1% rise in the index will cause the option price to increase by 10%.

It's as though I had invested ten times the amount that I actually did, so I'm controlling the equivalent of £50,000 of investment with only £5,000 at stake. Looking at it that way my maximum loss is only 10% of my notional £50,000 investment, not the 100% of £5,000 that you might have thought it was.

A sample list of options is given in Appendix B – Options Sample List.

Other Ways to Trade Straddles and Strangles
My 'options trading' is limited mainly to Covered Warrants, which to all intents are options in the traditional sense.

I also trade long and short via Listed Contracts for Difference (CFDs), and very occasionally via my spread trading account. Like options, these leveraged facilities also provide unlimited upside potential with limited downside potential. The downside is limited by the placing of mandatory stop orders at the level of the original investment. So you can never lose more than your original stake.

Despite the differences in the mechanics of covered warrants, listed CFDs, and spread bets; the techniques described in this chapter – straddles and strangles – may be equally applicable. With the following provisos:

- With Covered Warrants and Listed CFDs I must use straddles and strangles as a means of protection, because my stockbroker <u>does not</u> allow stop loss orders to be placed voluntarily on those instruments. Unlike ETFs.

- My spread trading account <u>does</u> allow me to place stop loss orders, so I can trade long or short using the techniques described in Chapter 3, without having to resort to straddles and strangles for protection.

- My spread trading account actually prohibits pure straddles. Setting up a short position, by selling an index, will cause any corresponding long position on the same index to be closed. And vice versa. I could work around this by taking simultaneous long- and short- positions on different but highly correlated indexes, or by establishing the short- and long- legs of the straddles using separate spread trading accounts.

Don't Lose Money!

Remember what I said at the outset: I'm not necessarily suggesting that you do trade both long and short on leveraged instruments. If you must, and you want some protection, you should...

Use Straddles and Strangles.

Chapter 7 – 'Don't Lose Money!' Trading System

In this chapter I'll summarize the techniques outlined in the previous chapters, and explore how they work together in the context of an overall 'trading system'; what I call the 'Don't Lose Money!' trading system.

First I'd like to set the scene by telling you what this book has really been about – 'money management'

About Money Management

According to Nassim Nicholas Taleb (in his book 'Fooled by Randomness') winning on the stock markets may in fact be more down to luck than skill. According to Michael Covel (in his book 'Trend Following'), and other authors on that subject, there's no point trying to predict the market but there is everything to gain by reacting to it.

The logical conclusion is that there is no secret strategy – no Holy Grail – for picking the right stocks, sectors, or companies to invest in. All you can do is buy and hope, and by sheer luck you'll have a 50% chance of being right.

Is it possible to make a profit if half your picks are winners and half are losers? Yes it is, providing you win more on the winners than you lose on the losers. You can do that by...

- Cutting your losers quickly, and letting your winners run.

Tony Loton

- Not trading with unfavorable bid-ask spreads and high transaction charges.

- Not getting wiped out by a single bad trade, so you can "stay in the game".

In a nutshell, even a 50% success rate in stock- or index-picking can yield a profit if you practice effective 'money management'.

Would you believe that the converse is also true?

Suppose you do have some special advantage that allows you to pick hot stocks 70% of the time. Can you still lose money? Yes you can.

As a concrete example, imagine that you purchase a 'hot stock' at a bid-ask spread of 4-5. If you need to sell out quickly, you've lost. If the stock rises, as predicted, by an impressive 10% – to a buy price of 5.5, sell price of 4.5 – you must still sell out at a loss; or hold for more gains. Suppose you hold out to see the selling price rise to 6 (a paper profit), you don't sell out, and it subsequently falls to 3. Again you were right (initially) that the stock would rise, but you still lost money – at least on paper. And most successful traders will tell you that paper losses are real losses.

Even with a stock picking advantage you could still make a net loss; by not winning as much on the winners as you lose on the losers; by not practicing effective money management.

That's really what this book has been about – money management.

Although my personal bias is towards index investing, coupled with technical market timing and trend following techniques, you should understand that good money management is also applicable to other – fundamental – approaches.

Was it not the fundamentalist Warren Buffett who inspired the title of this book?

The 'Don't Lose Money!' Trading System

The techniques described in the chapters of this book are all to do with money management and, taken together, comprise what I now call my 'Don't Lose Money!' trading system. I'll now summarize those techniques and explore how they work together in the context of the overall trading system comprising:

1. Trade Indexes, not Individual Stocks

2. Time the Market, Follow the Trend

3. Use Stops

4. Keep Trading Costs Low

5. Size Your Positions

6. Use Straddles and Strangles

What distinguishes this trading system from the 'get rich quick' trading systems you may have read about elsewhere is an acknowledgement of the *confirmation bias*. While positive examples are comforting, it takes an infinite number of positive results to really prove that a system works; yet only one negative result to prove that it doesn't. Beware the system that tells you what to do when things go right, but which leaves you high and dry when things go wrong.

Trade Indexes

The idea here is to lower risk: by providing diversity at lower cost than holding many stocks individually, while still allowing for a degree of specialization. For example, you could specialize in the Dow Jones (US), FTSE (UK), DAX (Germany), or even a property index.

Remember that the subsequent techniques do apply to individual stock holdings as well as indexes.

My suggestion was to hold indexes in the form of Exchange Traded Funds (ETFs) that offer lower trading costs and higher liquidity than traditional mutual funds.

By simply 'buying and holding' an index you won't outperform the market, but you won't underperform it either. But who says you have to buy and hold?

Time the Market, Follow the Trend

The idea here is to improve on 'average returns' by timing entries into the market (e.g. after major corrections) and riding the subsequent uptrend as long as possible until it runs out of steam. And to do that based on price action, with some appreciation of general market conditions, rather than based on stock fundamentals.

I find timing an entry into the market, to establish an initial position, to be the most difficult and frustrating aspect of trading. Once a position has been successfully established, the trend pretty much takes care of itself until your stop order is triggered.

Use Stops

The idea here is to limit losses, and protect profits, by applying stop orders to your holdings. It means you won't get wiped out if a trend suddenly reverses while you're not watching.

I highlighted the benefits of trailing stops (if your stockbroker provides them) and guaranteed stops (ditto), and I examined the issue of how tight to set those stops – not so tight that you get sold out on the slightest market 'noise', but tight enough to sell out at the first sign of real trouble.

Keep Trading Costs Low

The idea here is to guard against losing money routinely – even on potentially winning trades – by suffering high transaction costs, unfavorable bid-ask spreads, and avoidable taxes.

Size Your Positions

The idea here is to protect your capital by committing less when your confidence is low and more when your confidence is high; and to grow your positions, pyramiding as your confidence grows.

Use Straddles and Strangles

The idea here is to protect your positions in situations where you trade both ways (long and short), perhaps using leverage through options, and where your stockbroker does not provide the protection of stop orders.

That wasn't a recommendation to trade both ways, or to use leverage, but a way to protect yourself if you do.

More than the Sum of the Parts

You should see that those techniques are complementary, not mutually exclusive, and that a system combining some or all of the techniques should be more effective than any one technique. That is, the whole is more than the sum of the parts.

For example:

You can trade indexes using market timing / trend following techniques, with stop orders for protection, suffering low transaction charges, and committing the right amount of capital at the right time.

Or:

You can trade leveraged index options at times of high volatility, with the assurance that your strangle or straddle helps protect the downside while allowing for plenty of upside potential when the big move occurs.

Expect the Unexpected

The whole point of money management is to expect the unexpected. Not predict the unexpected, which by definition we can't, but prepare for it.

No matter how much homework you've done, there is always the possibility that your chosen stock – or the market as a whole – will suffer a sudden drop in price for reasons that you could not possibly predict. These 'black swan events', as Nassim Nicholas Taleb calls them, can work in a positive sense too, causing stocks or whole markets to rocket upwards for no apparent reason.

Our aim should be to stay in the market – at least to some degree – long enough to benefit from any expected or unexpected beneficial turn of events, but to get out (automatically) at the first sight of any unexpected detrimental turn of events.

Don't Lose Money (in the Stock Markets)

Such turns of events, booms and busts, through the ages have been well documented elsewhere. The 1929 Wall Street Crash springs to mind, as does the dot.com boom and the subsequent bust. Not to mention the property bubble that, as at September 2007, seems to have burst triggering a crisis in the US sub-prime lending market.

Indeed, on 7 September 2007 I read a news item reporting that Alan Greenspan, former Chairman of the Board of Governors of the Federal Reserve, had likened the most recent financial crisis to those former crises; including the one that I'll mention next.

I've suggested that good money management is not simply about minimizing risk. In fact, superficially minimizing risk might offer a false sense of security. Not only because it fails to capitalize from beneficial black swans, but because it fails to anticipate (not predict, or prevent) detrimental ones.

A good example of that is the spectacular collapse of Long Term Capital Management (LTCM) in 1998. While the LTCM hedge fund supposedly minimized risks by betting (both long and short) on the convergence of certain miss-priced securities, the strategy was based almost entirely on the premise that the market was a 'normal distribution'. The main protagonists – including Nobel-prize winners – discounted the possibility of outlying, unexpected events affecting the market and skewing that normal distribution. Specifically they failed to account for the Russian default in August 1998.

Thus the trading system that I have described in this book is underpinned by the notion that we should 'expect the unexpected'.

By adopting these techniques you might get rich, then again you might not, but at least you won't lose your shirt!

Chapter 8 – Beware...

In the previous chapters I've described my trading techniques for not losing money, and I've woven them in to an overall 'trading system'. That system suggests what you should do; not necessarily to get rich, but to at least to avoid getting poor.

It occurs to me that in my trading life I also incorporate some additional informal rules for what not to do. These are not positive steps you can take when placing or maintaining trades, but rather bad habits that you should not fall in to.

Each one is grounded in my personal experience.

Beware... Financial Advisers

In my pre-trading days I thought I was pretty savvy in taking advice from financial advisers and buying into the structured products they offered. When I say 'structured products' I mean pension schemes, long-term insurance plans, investment vehicles and the like.

The problem with such products is that they often came with high front-loaded charges (so that you wouldn't cash in straightaway) and little transparency as to how they actually worked. When those policies came to mature after the 'long term' (5, 10 years or even more) they would often be worth less than expected, and the original salesman would have long since retired to his Spanish villa; leaving no-one to complain to regarding the original 'advice'.

Those bad experiences provided the motivation I needed to get properly financially savvy, and to manage all of my investments myself. Surely I could make better decisions myself, and if I did succeed in losing everything – unlikely if I take my own advice in this book – then at least I'd have someone to blame; me!

It is true to say that these financial advisers – or salesmen, as I prefer to call them – do often have an impressive array of qualifications. But I have one qualification they don't have: I care about my own money.

I am reminded of a tongue-in-cheek definition I saw once for the term 'financial adviser'; or was it a 'stockbroker'?

"Someone who manages your money until it is all gone."

Obviously I do use a stockbroker, but on an execution-only basis. No investment advice is given, and none is required. I decide what to trade, and the broker carries out my instructions without question – usually in real time.

To add some balance, my 'financial advisor' reviewer of this book pointed out that there are some good advisors who offer transparent products with low charges. If you don't want the hassle of managing your own investments, you might be lucky enough to find one.

Beware... TV Pundits

In the UK there's a popular daily business show on TV. I tune in regularly; not only for the occasional nugget of good factual information, but also for the amusement value in watching the invited pundits pronouncing on the state of the markets.

One such regular pundit, employed by an impressive city investment firm, was Crazy Toby. Not his real name.

Don't Lose Money (in the Stock Markets)

When asked for his stock tips sometime in 2005, Crazy Toby recommended a particular stock. Each month he would be invited back on to the show, the host would gently point out that the stock had fallen – again, and Crazy Toby would say words to the effect "I still like this stock; good management etc.; stick with it or buy more". He said this without any apparent sense of irony, and each time it would fall some more. The host would invariably close each show by saying "Thanks as always Crazy Toby for your good advice".

What good advice?

Was Crazy Toby right? Actually he was right, and the stock did rise... eventually. Just as I might be right in continually pronouncing that "the market will crash". Yes it will, one day.

In the meantime you would have sat through many months holding a falling stock and not knowing if it would ever rise again. All that time your capital could have been invested elsewhere.

Beware... Financial News
As an experiment, I invite you to monitor the financial news sites for a week or so.

See how many times you see something like this:

14:30 Dow Jones falls on US Jobs Data

followed later in the day by...

15:15 Dow Jones rises on US Jobs Data

The problem is that financial journalists are paid to tell us not only 'what' is happening in the markets, but also 'why'; to establish cause-and-effect relationships whether they exist or not.

Tony Loton

In both cases those news headline may have been factually true. At 14:30 the Dow Jones index was falling on the day that US Jobs Data was announced. At 15:15 the market had rebounded, as it often does, also on the day that US Jobs Data was announced.

Surely, though, the US Jobs Data cannot be the cause of both the fall or the market and its subsequent rise.

I'm not trying to imply that financial news sites are of no value. I use them to establish the facts, but draw my own conclusions from those facts.

On news that interest rates have risen I might conclude that property prices are set for a fall... but not until the price action actually confirms my theory. And even then, I couldn't say with 100% certainty that "Property prices fall due to interest rate rise" thereby ruling out the other possibilities such as "Property prices fall due to new tax regime" or "Property prices fall due to unexpected rise in unemployment".

Beware... Free Trading Seminars
Skeptical as I am, I've always steered clear of these. My suspicions, confirmed by the apocryphal tales I've heard, are that they are little more than sales seminars for £1,000 training courses promising untold riches.

All well and good if the tutor really is a trading god, but how do you know until you've stumped up the cash? Think how many trading books you could buy with that money; which brings me to...

Beware... Authors of Trading Books
Yes, that includes me. How ironic.

Don't Lose Money (in the Stock Markets)

There are numerous theories on how to beat the market, each backed by one or more very credible published works. They can't all be right; or maybe they can, but not for you.

Trading and investing is as much about your own personal psychology, and personal circumstances, as it is about following a set of one-size-fits all rules. For someone with inexhaustible patience and lots of cash the long-term 'buy and hold' value investing approach might just work. For someone with less patience and bills to pay (yes, it's me) that approach just won't suit.

My closing advice is:

Read everything you can about trading and investment, but don't reach any conclusions about any particular approach until you have tried it for yourself. And don't do that without a trading safety net; without a set of techniques to ensure you won't lose it all.

This book is my trading safety net.

It might not make you rich, but at least you won't lose your shirt!

Don't Lose Money!

Appendix A – ETFs Sample List

To show the range of indexes, and other pooled investments, that can be traded via Exchange Traded Funds (ETFs) I have listed here a subset of the iShares ETFs that are available to me at the time of writing. This list is growing all the time (see www.ishares.co.uk and www.ishares.com), and there are other ETF providers such as ProShares (www.proshares.com).

There's plenty of scope here to diversify, yet specialize at the same time; but I must stress that I am merely listing these, not recommending them.

Developed Equity
FTSE 100 (code ISF), S&P 500 (code IUSA), MSCI Japan (code IJPN), MSCI World (code IWRD), AEX (code IAEX), MSCI Europe ex UK (code IEUX), MSCI North America (code INAA), MSCI Europe (code IMEU), S&P / MIB (code IMIB).

Equity-Income
DJ Euro STOXX Select Dividend (code IDVY), FTSE UK Dividend Plus (code IUKD), DJ Asia / Pacific Select Dividend (code IAPD).

Emerging Equity
FTSE / Xinhua CHINA 25 (code FXC), MSCI AC Far East ex Japan (code IFFF), MSCI Emerging Markets (code IEEM), MSCI Eastern Europe (code IEER), MSCI Taiwan (code ITWN), MSCI Korea (code IKOR), MSCI Brazil (code IBZL), MSCI Turkey (code ITKY), FTSE BRIC 50 (code BRIC).

Property

FTSE / EPRA European Property Index Fund (code IPRP), FTSE EPRA / NAREIT Asia Property Yield Fund (code IASP), FTSE EPRA / NAREIT Global Property Yield Fund (code IWDP), FTSE EPRA / NAREIT US Property Yield Fund (code IUSP), FTSE EPRA / NAREIT UK Property Fund (code IUKP).

Appendix B – Options Sample List

In order to provide a sample range of leveraged options that may be traded in the form of Covered Warrants or Listed Contracts for Difference (LCFDs, which are not strictly options), I have listed here a subset of those available through my stockbroker at the time of writing.

I've listed examples of CWs and LCFDs for the Dow Jones Industrial Average and FTSE 250 indexes because those lists are quite manageable. I can tell you that in addition there were about 30 options available to me on the FTSE 100 at the time of writing.

As before, I'm merely listing these, not recommending them.

Dow Jones Industrial Average

STRIKE PRICE	EXPIRY DATE	CALL / PUT	CW / LCFD
12,000	21-Dec-2007	CALL	CW
14,000	**21-Dec-2007**	**CALL**	**CW**
12,000	**21-Dec-2007**	**PUT**	**CW**
13,000	19-Dec-2008	CALL	CW
15,000	19-Dec-2008	CALL	CW

The objective is to find a CALL – PUT pair with the same expiry date, and the nearest strike prices either side of the current market price. With the Dow Jones today sitting around 13,000, the two entries shown bold would fit the bill; but beware that in that case the base of the strangle would be 2,000 points wide. That's a 15% (of the current DJ price) window in which you stand to lose money.

Now, if the Dow Jones index was currently sitting at 12,000 you would be able to establish a perfect straddle by utilizing the 12,000 CALL and the 12,000 PUT both of which have the same expiry date of 21-Dec-2007.

FTSE 250

STRIKE PRICE	EXPIRY DATE	CALL / PUT	CW / LCFD
12,850	12-Oct-2007	PUT	LCFD
13,370	12-Oct-2007	PUT	LCFD
13,500	12-Oct-2007	PUT	LCFD
9,850	11-Jan-2008	CALL	LCFD
13,000	20-Jun-2008	CALL	CW
14,000	20-Jun-2008	CALL	CW
15,000	20-Jun-2008	CALL	CW
12,000	20-Jun-2008	PUT	CW
11,000	21-Sep-2007	CALL	CW
12,000	21-Sep-2007	CALL	CW
13,000	21-Sep-2007	CALL	CW
10,000	21-Sep-2007	PUT	CW

Don't Lose Money (in the Stock Markets)

It should be apparent that the FTSE 250 table provides a wider set of possibilities for establishing straddles and strangles; actually, more than I've listed.

I'll leave it up to you to figure out how you could best utilize them.

Bibliography

In the past few years I have read as many trading and investing books as I could lay my hands on; covering all approaches from fundamental value-investing to purely technical trading, on timescales from short term (trading) to long-term (investing).

Having tried the various approaches with varying degrees of success, I have now whittled that long list down to the few books given special mention in this work.

Those books are:

Cohen, Guy; Options Made Easy; FT Press; 2005

Darvas, Nicholas; How I Made $2 Million in the Stock Market; Harriman House; 2007

Darvas, Nicholas; Wall Street - The Other Las Vegas; Lyle Stuart; 2002

Gunther, Max; The Zurich Axioms; Souvenir Press; 1985

Lefevre, Edwin; Reminiscences of a Stock Operator; Wiley; 1998

Masonson, Leslie N; All About Market Timing; McGraw Hill; 2004

Soros, George; The Alchemy of Finance; Wiley; 2003

Teleb, Nassim Nicholas; The Black Swan; Penguin; 2007

Teleb, Nassim Nicholas; Fooled by Randomness; Random House; 2007

Tharp, Van K.; Trade Your Way to Financial Freedom;
McGraw Hill; 1999

Don't Lose Money (in the Stock Markets)

Index

correction, 27, 28, 29, 35, 37, 49

Covel, Michael, 24, 65

covered warrants, 23, 55

Covered Warrants, 23, 62, 63

credit crunch, 1

Darvas, Nicholas, 3, 24, 37

DAX, 2, 15

diversification, 7

diversify, 7, 16

dividend, 12

don't lose money, 23, 36, 52

Don't Lose Money, i, 1, 17, 25, 30, 38, 45, 54, 63, 65

dot.com, 9, 11

Dow Jones, 2, 8, 9, 10, 11, 15, 34, 44, 56, 59

Dow Jones industrial Average, 25

ETF, 28, 39, 40, 44

ETFs, 13, 14, 33, 39, 40, 42, 55, 63

Exchange Traded Funds, 13, 14, 33

exercise, 60

expectation, 48, 54

Experience Note, 5, 9, 27, 37, 43, 53, 61

Don't Lose Money (in the Stock Markets)

mutual funds, 13, 14

noise, 36, 50, 54

options, 55, 56, 57, 58, 60, 61, 62

outperformers, 10

portfolio, 41, 42

position sizing, 47, 52

premium, 56, 57

profit, 25, 28, 31, 33, 36, 44, 51, 52, 54

profits, 31, 33, 35, 44, 50

ProShares, 14

PUT, 56, 57, 58, 59, 60, 61

regular trading account, 23

Regular trading account, 32, 37

risk, 10, 12, 15, 16, 20, 32, 34, 41

rolling bets, 16

saw tooth, 25

Self Invested Personal Pension, 13

short, 4, 21, 23, 25, 29, 30, 35, 51, 55, 56, 62, 63

SIPP, 13, 23, 32, 37, 41, 42, 44, 55

Soros, George, 49

speculating, 4, 23, 55

Don't Lose Money (in the Stock Markets)

Lightning Source UK Ltd.
Milton Keynes UK
28 August 2009

143145UK00002B/150/P

9 780955 676406